MASTER PLAN

INTEGRATING
YOUR FINANCIAL PLANNING,
LEGAL AND ESTATE PLANNING
AND LIFE PLANNING

BYRON E. WOODMAN, JR.
MICHAEL T. HARTLEY

Cultivating Change® LLC
101 West Venice Avenue, Suite 10
Venice, FL 34285
941.480.1119 telephone
941.484.5702 facsimile
cultivatingchange.com website
info@cccll.com email

©2006 by Byron E. Woodman, Jr. and Michael T. Hartley

No portion of this book may be reproduced in any medium without the written permission of the publisher.

Cultivating Change® LLC is not engaged in rendering legal, financial, therapeutical or other professional services. If expert assistance is required, the services of a competent professional person should be sought.

Second Edition, September 2006
ISBN 0-9785517-3-5

Printed and distributed by Cambio Press LLC.

Dedication

To our instructors and mentors, as well as the many clients and organizations who have given us the wonderful opportunity to serve them. Through our relationships with them, we have learned the strategies that we now have the joy of sharing for the benefit of others.

Acknowledgements

The development of this book has been a collaborative effort that has stretched across our professional practices. To all those mentioned and all those unmentioned, we express our deep appreciation and gratitude.

Our clients have provided us with inspiration and have been stimulating and fun members of our teams.

Kelvey Woodman and Bonnie Brown Hartley have encouraged and guided us with their personal and professional insights. They have provided invaluable assistance with content, organization and editing as well as lots of patience.

Many people in our respective offices have shaped our thinking. At Woodman & Eaton, they include attorneys William Eaton, Peter Johnson, Mark Huffman and Laurel Millette. A special thanks goes to Byron's assistant, Pamela Dixon, and other members of his administrative staff. At Dale K. Ehrhart, Inc., help came from Michael W. Hartley, Robert Keyser, James Moore, Kathy Newsome, Marcy O'Neil, and Byron Sanders.

People who have guided us in developing clarity about the major concepts presented in this book include Dan Sullivan, David Booth, Kenneth R. French, Eugene Fama Jr., David Butler, Robert Esperti, Renno Peterson, and Robert J. Petrossi.

People whose work we have looked to and built upon include James. E. Hughes Jr., Peter L. Bernstein, Jane Hilburt-Davis, and Charles W. Collier.

Colleagues, over the years, have helped us develop concepts and experience. Many of them have worked in teams with us. Although we cannot name all of them, some who merit recognition are: Michael Tillman, JD, Robert Goldman, JD, Edward S. Heald, Stephen R. Dooley, JD, CPA, Patricia M. Annino, JD, Jill Lervold, CPA, Marshall Jones, JD, CLU, Thomas E. Peckham, JD, LLM, Darrell Canby, CPA, CFP, Tony Anchukaitis, CPA,

Scott Tansey, JD, LLM, Thom Rodgers, JD, William Payne, CLU, Dan Guglielmo, JD, Ralph Heckert, Elaine L. Bonoma, CFP, Richard Breed, JD, Tim Gibson, CLU, Roy M. Henshaw, CPA, John H. Kellogg, JD, Vonya Lance, JD, LLM, Dee Lee, CFP, Richard G. Nelson, CPA, Asa E. Phillips, III, JD, Carol E. Tully, JD, CPA, Robert L. DeGregorio, Tom Bishop, CFP, CLU, Jonathan C. Wolff, CLU, Sidney F. Greeley, Jr., CLU, and Lynne Bernfield, MA, MFCT.

Also meriting recognition as fellow students and colleagues of these principals are members of WealthCounsel, LLC, The Family Firm Institute, Attorneys for Family-Held Enterprises, The Family Business Network, and The Family Legacy Network.

Finally, but not least, the professionals who have assisted us in preparing and editing the manuscript, including Susan Weiner, Jerril Nilson, Bill Bishop and Linda Cashdan and the crew who have accomplished the production of the book.

Table of Contents

Dedication 3

Acknowledgements 4

Introduction: Creating the Missing Magic 9
    The Sullivan Family
    Max Hatfield, Executor of Father's Estate
    Marjorie Lambert, Widowed Professional
    How the Magic of a Master Plan Can Help You

Chapter One: The Integrated Planning Process™ 15
    Pre-Stage – Getting Acquainted
    Stage 1 – Evaluation
    Stage 2 – Goals Development
    Stage 3 – Plan Design
    Stage 4 – Implementation
    Stage 5 – Plan Oversight and Governance

Chapter Two: The Risks of an Unintegrated Approach 23
    The "No Huddle Trap"
    The Dangers of "Boxcar Planning"
    Three Risks to You and Your Family
    Why Isolated and Narrowly Focused Advice Does Not Work

Chapter Three: Establishing a Team 27
    The Process for Creating Teams
    Overview of Team's Role
    Team Leadership
    Why Having a Team is Key

Chapter Four: The Three Types of Capital 33
    The Wealth Cycle
    The Three Types of Capital
    Plan for All Three Types of Capital
    Thinking about Financial Capital
    Thinking about Social Capital
    Thinking about Human Capital

Chapter Five: Integrated Planning Process 43
    The Tone of the Relationship (Chemistry)
    Pre-Engagement Stage – Getting Acquainted
    Stage 1 – Evaluation

Chapter Six: Integrated Planning Process: Stage 2 – Goals Development 49
    The Importance of Goals Development
    The Sub-Goal Trap
    Vision vs. Goals

Chapter Seven: Integrated Planning Process: Goals Development Case Study 53
    The Young Family
    The Retired Family
    Questions that Can Uncover Your Vision and Goals
    Two Strategic Tools
    Thinking Strategically

Chapter Eight: Integrated Planning Process: Stage 3 – Plan Design and Stage 4 – Implementation 63
    Take a Holistic Approach
    Developing Your Detailed Plan
    Your Participation
    Implementation

Chapter Nine: Integrated Planning Process: Stage 5 – Plan Oversight and Governance 69
    Your Role and Your Family's Role in Stage 5
    Your Team's Role
    Helpful Processes
    Judging Your Team's Effectiveness

Chapter Ten: The Benefits of a Fully Functioning Integrated Plan 77

Afterword 80

A Comment about Fees 81

Information about the Authors 82

Selected Readings 84

Introduction
Creating the Missing Magic with a Master Plan

Individuals or families with significant net worth may seem to outsiders to have everything they could wish for. The reality is far more complex.

In fact, many high net worth families fail to achieve the life and legacy they desire because they do not integrate their financial, legal and life planning. The following fictitious examples illustrate this challenge.

The Sullivan Family

Robert Sullivan and his wife Kitty had two adult children and all the material things they could desire: a thriving family business that they hope to pass on to future generations, a beautiful house in the city, and a stunning country estate. Their net worth of more than $10 million afforded them significant involvement in community and charitable projects that gave them tremendous satisfaction.

However, when Bob and Kitty sat down for a heart to heart talk, they realized they shared some big picture concerns.

- **Children**. They worried that their children, Thomas and Marisa, did not share the family's traditional values of hard work, persistence, and community service. Especially they feared that Thomas felt too entitled, valued material things too much, and would not properly manage his inheritance.
- **Effective Management of Financial and Legal Affairs**. They felt they wasted too much time meeting with their many advisers: three lawyers, an accountant, a financial adviser, a life insurance adviser, and a property/casualty insurance agent. As their affairs became more complex, they felt frustrated that no single adviser understood the entire picture well enough to spot a missing element. For example, they recently learned they had missed an opportunity to save on their taxes using a capital loss. This happened because their attorney failed to tell their financial adviser about their plan to gift some partnership units in their family limited partnership to their children. They wondered if there was a more efficient way to manage things.
- **Long-Term Goals**. While Bob and Kitty were happy that they had built a robust business and raised two smart, healthy children, they wanted their lives to have more meaning and a sense of direction.

Max Hatfield, Executor of Father's Estate

When his father, Jake, died, Max Hatfield learned that his father's army of advisers—including top corporate lawyers, well-known money managers, and a leading accounting firm—had not helped Jake as much as they could have in handling his estate consisting of real estate, equities, intellectual property, and private corporations.

Here's what Max found:

- **Unnecessarily onerous taxes**. Jake's will was woefully outdated, many of the real estate assets were not properly titled, and the three investment portfolios had not been properly coordinated. As a result of this lack of coordination between advisers, estate and income taxes consumed more than 65 percent of the estate's $55 million value.

- **No lasting legacy.** Max felt sad because his father's will did not include final words of wisdom for his family and other beneficiaries. Max knew his father was not big on face-to-face conversations. "If only Dad had written something down," he said. None of Jake's advisers asked him what he wanted to leave as his personal legacy.

Marjorie Lambert, Widowed Professional

Marjorie Lambert, M.D. thought of herself as a leader. A former high school field hockey team captain, Marjorie led a team of cardiologists at one of New England's leading hospitals. She had also raised five sons and managed most household tasks. But when her husband died suddenly, Marjorie started to question her abilities.

Why did Marjorie question herself?

- **Difficulty grasping family finances.** It was time-consuming to meet individually with the family's many advisers—lawyers about the estate plan, investment manager about the portfolio, and insurance agent about life and casualty policies. Moreover, Marjorie simply didn't have the skills or time to understand the overall situation. More alarming, none of her advisors got the big picture. She wished that her husband had either left more detailed instructions, or had enlisted a professional who had a command of all their financial affairs.

- **Advisers who don't collaborate.** During the following six months, Marjorie tried to get her advisers to work together, but nothing seemed to work. She wished she could find an expert who would help her put it all together. However, she had no idea where to find such a person, or if such a person existed.

Each of these examples illustrates a significant and common problem facing wealthy families and individuals like you. But you don't have to suffer the same distress as the Sullivans, Max Hatfield, or Marjorie Lambert.

How the Magic of a Master Plan Can Help You

We call our solution "magic" for the way it has benefited our clients' lives. Our integrated *Master Plan* approach to planning empowers you to accomplish many financial and legal tasks more efficiently. You will learn to better understand your investment portfolio and estate plan, prepare your heirs for their inheritance, and plan your philanthropic and charitable activities.

Even better, the concepts and tools described in *Master Plan* free you to focus more on achieving your life goals, incorporating them into a set of family goals. You will feel more confident making decisions about your wealth and your family because you will have a master plan.

This book can help you:

- Establish an **advisory team** of professionals and family members who work in harmony to provide your family with integrated financial and legal advice focused on your priorities, while making the best use of your time

- Develop an **integrated financial, legal and life plan** that your team will help you to maintain and adapt as your situation changes

- Provide inspiration for your loved ones—and involve your children—by developing and implementing a **family vision and goals statement**

- **Live your life to the fullest** and enjoy using your personal and financial strengths for the benefit of yourself, your family and your world

You will learn to reach these goals using the *Integrated Planning Process*™.

If you are a financial or legal professional, this book can help you to deliver a more satisfying experience to your clients.

Peace of mind can result from the collective efforts of families and their advisory teams. Turn to Chapter One to start your journey toward creating your *Master Plan*.

KEY CONCEPT

- An integrated approach to financial, legal and life planning can help you and your family avoid pitfalls and live more fulfilling lives.

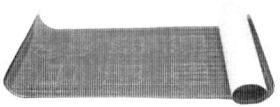

Chapter One
The Integrated Planning Process™ Begin With the End in Mind

You'll create the most successful integrated plan if you "begin with the end in mind," to quote Steven Covey, author of *The Seven Habits of Highly Effective People*. In other words, you need to understand your big picture goals for your family before you start planning. This is a very powerful starting point.

You will find that peace of mind flows from having:

- A clear direction and control
- Confidence that your plan will accomplish your family's goals
- The capabilities needed to accomplish your goals
- A plan that adapts to changing circumstances

The Integrated Planning Process is based on the assumption that you must understand where you're going before you can develop an effective plan. As you see in Table I, it starts with *Evaluation* followed by *Goals Development*, then *Plan Design*, *Implementation*, and finally, *Plan Oversight and Governance*.

The Integrated Planning Process™

STAGES	VALUE CREATED	YOUR COMMITMENT	YOU RECEIVE	WHO IS INVOLVED
Pre-Engagement Stage	Family and advisory team find out if they are a good fit	Provide basic summary information about present situation and participate in a 2–4 hour meeting	Orientation about planning techniques and the Integrated Planning Process	Initial planning team and family decision-makers
Evaluation	Awareness of current situation and array of available planning alternatives	Provide complete information about assets, liabilities and current legal plans	Clear information about your current situation	You, your spouse and lead advisers
Goals Development	Clarity regarding family goals and ways an Integrated Planning Process can help achieve them	Engage in activities designed to clearly describe goals and objectives	Benefit from your introspection and the comfort of having clearly defined Goals Statement	You, your spouse and lead advisers
Plan Design	Financial and legal plans designed to achieve specific family goals	Interact with advisory team providing responses to design iterations; learn about new strategies	Design Book and orientation to the design and its legal and investment strategies	You, your spouse and lead advisers and additional advisers for special projects
Implementation	Plan is funded and investment policies are written and employed	Execute all documents required to put plan into effect	Progress reports and copy of completed Integrated Plan	You, your spouse and lead advisers and additional advisers for special projects
Plan Oversight and Governance	Tax matters are monitored; investment accounts are monitored and rebalanced; legal formalities of the Plan are observed and documented; Plan is adapted over time to changing conditions	You review periodic reports; execute authorizations to keep Plan in operation	Periodic reports and presentations at meetings regarding the operation of your Integrated Plan	You, your spouse and other lead family members, and lead advisers

The Integrated Planning Process table also shows:

- The value created for your family
- Your contribution to each stage
- The deliverables you receive at each stage
- Who is involved in each stage

Pre-Engagement Stage – Getting Acquainted

For you and your team to work well together, you must get acquainted before you begin the five stages of integrated planning. The *Pre-Engagement Stage* is a period of mutual discovery. You educate your team about your family. The team educates you about the benefits and requirements of the *Integrated Planning Process*.

Stage 1 – Evaluation

In the *Evaluation Stage* your team reviews copies of your current planning documents (wills, trusts, insurance policies, business agreements, deeds, tax returns, etc.) and information about all of your assets and liabilities. Then they analyze your current plan to assess how well it serves you.

In the *Evaluation Stage* your team uncovers risks as well as opportunities for improvement. This preliminary understanding of your circumstances, including family dynamics, is critical for you and your advisers. It will make you productive in the *Goals Development Stage*.

Stage 2 – Goals Development

An effective integrated plan starts with a clear set of goals. During a detailed discussion, you and your team gather the information that enables you and your team to write a concise set of goals that touch on all three forms of family wealth.

The three forms of family wealth to plan for are:

- Financial capital (what you own);
- Social capital (how you relate to society through volunteering, taxes and philanthropy); and
- Human capital (your knowledge, stories, values, skills, intellectual capital and wisdom, and members of your family and the people who are important to them). Human capital is also the informal family systems and the more formalized governance protocols that families sometimes create to manage decision-making and relationships.

You'll read more about these three types of capital in Chapter Four.

So you can plan appropriately, be clear about what you want for yourself and your heirs. Consider the following questions:

- How much, when, and what types of property?
- What types of education?
- What types of travel experiences?
- What lessons about life, leadership, honor, integrity and charity?
- How will the family work together harmoniously—now and when you are not around?

The human capital portion of your wealth can be the most important to the long-term success of your heirs and beneficiaries, and at the same time may be the most difficult to pass on.

The success of your plan depends on getting the right amount and type of capital to the right people at the right time.

A draft of your Goals Statement is provided to you for review, comment and modification. Once you approve it, the planning and design process begins.

Stage 3 – Plan Design

In the *Plan Design Stage*, your advisers, working together as a design team, begin to create the architecture of your integrated financial and estate plan.

The design team will probably establish a hypothesis about the kind of plan required by your unique circumstances. The team may also create a computer model that incorporates the unique financial, legal and tax characteristics of each element of the plan. Your team will then test the design with a variety of assumptions including asset growth rates, cash flow and spending rates, inflation rates, and tax and expense structures.

As a part of the design process, financial strategies may be developed for each element of your plan. Investment portfolios may be tailored to accommodate variations in cash flow demands, tax structures, and the need for reaching specific growth targets to accomplish the results contemplated for each legal structure.

A proposed plan will be presented to you for review and comment. In response to your comments, your advisers may adjust the plan before proceeding to the *Implementation Stage*.

Stage 4 – Implementation

In the *Implementation Stage*, once you have settled on a design for your family's financial and legal future, thoughtful and effective implementation must occur.

In order to achieve the long-term benefits contemplated by the plan, legal formalities must be carefully observed.

Documents that will be executed to establish new entities (such as trusts, family limited partnerships, and charitable structures) should contain language that reflects the state-of-the-art in legal document drafting. Specified assets will then be re-titled so that they are owned by the proper entities of your plan. This is the *Funding Process* portion of the *Implementation Stage*.

Also in this stage, your team will establish the systems and procedures that will enable the next stage—*Plan Oversight and Governance*—to be accomplished efficiently.

Stage 5 – Plan Oversight and Governance

Plan Oversight and Governance begins as your plan is implemented. It involves numerous formalities that ensure that you and your family receive the plan's benefits throughout your lifetimes.

The complicated give-and-take required to monitor and maintain an integrated financial and legal plan can seem daunting. The members of your team will insulate you from much of that. They will translate complexity into understandable terms, to increase your confidence and control. When the members of your team serve with you in this capacity, we refer to them as *The Family Board of Directors*®[1] or *The Family Board of Advisors*™. For the sake of simplicity, this book uses the term *"Family Board"* in place of the preceding two names. In all cases it refers to a team of advisers and lead family members selected by the primary family leaders. The Family Board is discussed in detail in Chapter Nine.

The *Plan Oversight and Governance* systems bring a degree of institutional organization to your family's affairs so that the members of your family can focus on what is really important—your lives!

Still not convinced that you need to integrate your financial, legal and life planning? Then proceed to Chapter Two, *The Risks of an Unintegrated Approach*.

Do you like the idea of taking an integrated approach, but you are not sure you have the right team members? Chapter Three, *Establishing a Team*, will answer your questions.

If you are sure you have the right team, then proceed to Chapter

---

[1]"The Family Board of Directors" was conceived by Michael T. Hartley and is a registered trademark of Tillman Hartley LLC.

Four, *The Three Types of Capital*, to learn about these important concepts underlying the Magic of an *Integrated Planning Process* tailored to your unique needs and circumstances.

Key Concepts

- The Integrated Planning Process is a systematic approach to achieving your big picture goals for your family.

- The success of your plan depends on getting the right amount and type of capital to the right people at the right time.

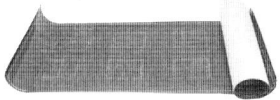

Chapter Two
The Risks of an Unintegrated Approach

High net-worth individuals and families usually hire first-class advisers. However, they often fail to achieve superior results. Why? Because their team is not coordinated. The price of failure may be high in terms of financial and personal opportunities.

The "No Huddle Trap"

When you and your advisers act without an integrated financial and legal plan, you are like a football team playing without a huddle or a playbook. During the game, each player does what he or she does best, but without regard for the other players' actions. As a result, the quarterback throws the ball toward the goal posts, but the receiver is not there because he was not told where to go. Despite an extremely talented coach and players, the team fails to score a touchdown. We call this the "No Huddle Trap."

Most families with more than $10 million dollars in assets lack an **integrated** financial and legal plan to achieve their goals. In many cases, they cannot even state their goals clearly, so they have no way to measure whether they are making progress. As a result, they drift along at the mercy of events and well-intentioned advisers who may pull them in different directions.

The Dangers of "Boxcar Planning"

Even if your advisers do work together, you can still run into trouble if they tackle issues only as they arise. Your family's financial and legal structures will be created in a hodgepodge manner.

For example, a particular investment may be selected because it appears hot; a revocable living trust may be established to avoid probate in the future; a charitable trust may be set up to avoid capital gains on a highly appreciated asset. You end up with a string of unrelated strategies, like boxcars of potatoes, lumber and widgets added to the end of a train. We call this "Boxcar Planning."

Over time, this string of strategies loses direction and becomes cumbersome. You may begin to feel out of control and uncertain about your family's direction. That's why it is important to have your coach, a huddle and a playbook.

Three Risks to You and Your Family

Without a well-coordinated plan for your family's legal and financial affairs, you run three serious risks.

First, loss of financial capital because you:

- Have not optimized your tax planning
- Take unnecessary risks in your investment portfolio(s)
- Lack a creditor protection plan

Second, family members don't achieve their full potential because you:

- Do not have an integrated plan to pass on your values, traditions, skills, and wisdom
- Have not prepared your heirs to manage their current and future wealth

Third, your family fails to achieve its goals because you:

- Have not established clear goals
- Do not have an integrated plan or the family systems to achieve those goals
- Have not prepared your heirs to work together harmoniously

Why Isolated and Narrowly Focused Advice Does Not Work

The most common mistake made by wealthy families is employing numerous advisers who do not work as a team. This often happens because they have gathered advisers as needs arise. For example, they may have engaged several attorneys for separate transactions, one accounting firm for their family business and another for their personal taxes, and several investment managers.

When advisers lack an overall picture of a family's circumstances or goals, they cannot do the best job possible. Each adviser's actions may seem appropriate in isolation. However, they may actually be working at cross purposes.

For example, a well-intentioned investment adviser wasted a charitable deduction carry-forward. She eagerly harvested losses at year-end, unaware that the large charitable deduction carry-forward was in its last year. She should have been realizing gains to be offset by the deduction. An excellent opportunity was missed due to lack of communication with her client's accountant.

Without a comprehensive plan with clearly defined goals for your advisers to work from, it is difficult to detect actions that work at cross-purposes or to gauge progress.

Twenty-five years ago, we recognized that a fragmented approach wasn't effective for clients with complex financial and legal needs. So we broke new ground by bringing together our clients' advisers to work as a team. We—and our clients—discovered the Magic that resulted from integrated financial, legal and life planning. A team approach generates better ideas and more efficient implementation of strategies. That's because each team member works in a coordinated way and focuses on the client's overall personal and financial goals.

This experience has allowed us to refine our ideal of how integrated financial and legal planning should work. In the chapters that follow, you will learn about the process through which you can achieve superior results for your family.

Key Concepts

- An unintegrated approach to financial, legal and life planning may cause your family to miss financial and personal opportunities. Capable advisers may work at cross-purposes because they are ill-informed about your overall situation.

- Your financial and legal advisers can achieve the best results for you when they work with you as part of an integrated team. An integrated team will give you greater confidence and control.

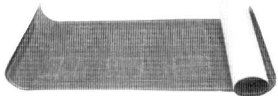

Chapter Three
Establishing a Team

So, you want to take an integrated approach to your financial, legal and life planning. Where do you start?

The first step is to assemble a team. "A team is a small number of people with complementary skills who are committed to a common purpose, performance goals, and approach for which they hold themselves mutually accountable."[2] They will work in harmony to provide you with the benefit of their combined skill, judgment, expertise and wisdom. Mutual respect and trust among team members will be necessary for the relationships to flourish.

Your team will consist of family members and professional advisers. Some of the professional advisers will be called "lead" or "primary" advisers because of their central role in your planning process. One of the lead advisers will serve as a team leader to coordinate activities, as discussed under "Team Leadership."

---

[2] Jon R. Katzenbach and Douglas K. Smith, The Wisdom of Teams (McKinsey & Company, Inc., 1993)

The Process for Creating Teams

You will start your integrated planning team with your existing advisers. For example, your team of advisers may include your:

- CPA
- Investment adviser
- Financial planner
- Estate planning attorney
- Life or casualty insurance advisers
- Trust officers
- Junior family members
- Other family consultants

Teams will differ according to your family's needs and the capabilities of your advisers, especially their willingness to work in team situations.

When necessary, you and your lead advisers will choose new members. As with a sports team, you will select them for their ability to "play the position" the team requires as measured by their technical expertise and ability to work effectively with your other team members.

As the need arises, you may introduce a new team member to provide a specialized service that you do not need on an ongoing basis. Once that service is complete, the team member withdraws, but remains available as a resource.

For example, once your team completes your plan and creates the appropriate entities, you may ask an expert in property, casualty and liability insurance to review the insurance coverage for each entity for gaps and overlaps. After you have evaluated and acted on those recommendations, the expert may withdraw from active participation on your team, but would still be available to review future liability issues.

Overview of Team's Role

Once the professional team is engaged, all members must invest their time to ensure that they clearly understand your family's circumstances and goals.

The members of the team develop the operating and governance protocols for the team and communicate clearly and in a timely manner throughout the engagement. Specific communication tools are provided, including computer-based collaboration tools, private intranets, conference servers, digital document storage, and management systems.

With participation from the appropriate team members, they develop financial models that allow you to evaluate strategies. You can also use these models to measure progress over time. When your family circumstances change, they will help identify how to modify your plans.

Team Leadership

Your team leader will act as your team's quarterback, playing an essential role in making the *Integrated Planning Process* work.

For you and your family to feel confident that someone other than you can guide and control your family's financial, legal and life planning process, you must feel confidence in the leader of your team.

Selection of your team leader depends on what works for you and your family. You, your family, or team members may select the leader, or the leader may be selected by mutual agreement.

The team leader functions like the general contractor on a home-building project. The general contractor must communicate with the family, architects and the various subcontractors and make sure that everybody shows up at the right place, at the right time and does the job according to expectations.

The leader might not be the person whom you have traditionally considered your most important adviser. Indeed, often that adviser prefers not to take on the time-consuming role of team leader for complex estates.

Instead, the leader will be the team member who thoroughly understands your family's issues and goals and who has the skills, time and sense of responsibility needed for the team to function well. Furthermore, the team leader must be given enough support so that he or she can delegate certain aspects of the leadership and follow-up.

It is likely that the team leadership will rotate among the various members of the team as you enter different stages of the *Integrated Planning Process*. For example, one member may lead during the initial *Evaluation* and *Goals Development* stages. Another member may lead during *Design and Implementation*. Leadership for *Plan Oversight and Family Governance*, the final stage, is likely to return to the team member who led the *Evaluation* and *Goals Development* stages. Also family members may provide leadership for some aspects of the planning, such as business succession.

The tasks of the leader vary depending upon the stage of the process. Some of the elements of a leader's job description are listed in the shaded box. Note that the team leader may delegate many of these items, but must retain responsibility for making sure they are completed.

Team Leader's Responsibilities

- **Receive and manage answers to family member questions.** Be available to handle the family's questions and comments whenever they arise. Distribute questions and comments among the team members for appropriate responses and make sure that the answers are delivered in a timely fashion to the family.
- **Take initiative to coordinate.** Must be well organized and willing to take initiative to accomplish the family goals.
- **Establish a time line.** Schedule and coordinate meeting dates, locations and facilities so all team members are available for those dates
- **Agenda.** Establish the agenda for each meeting
- **Arrange for minutes.** Identify someone to take minutes of the meeting, prepare and circulate draft minutes to be reviewed for accuracy by the team members and, soon after the meeting, distribute the minutes to the family members for review and approval
- **Team follow-up.** Follow up with the various team members regarding their respective assigned responsibilities to make sure that everybody is doing what they should do and staying on schedule
- **Pre-meeting preparation.** Call for the pre-meeting discussion among the professional team members in preparation for meetings with the family

When new teams include members who have not previously worked together, it is often helpful for the group to do some team training to ensure they have the right expectations and skills to be effective team members.[3]

---

[3] We use a process called the Accelerated Business Team™ to facilitate team effectiveness. In this process the team members learn team protocols and how to use the technology platforms designed to support communication.

Why Having a Team is a Key to Success

Taking an integrated team approach will make you feel:

- **Relieved** to lean on team support as you deal with the burdens and complexity of wealth
- **Confident** that you are in charge
- **Satisfied** that your team leader will take on the responsibility—and devote the time necessary—to coordinate the team based on your wishes
- **Grateful** that you can enhance your support to family members as they seek to live happy and productive lives and develop new skills, strengths, and competencies

Supporting your family members is not just a matter of money. Sometimes the best kind of support is non-financial, as you will learn in the next chapter on the three types of capital.

KEY CONCEPTS

- A team is a small number of people with complementary skills who are committed to a common purpose, performance goals, and approach for which they hold themselves mutually accountable.
- Assemble your team according to your family's needs and the capabilities of your existing family advisers.
- The team leader will be responsible for the coordination and smooth operation of the team.
- Some team members may be involved only on a project basis as needed.

Chapter Four
The Three Types of Capital

It is very important to focus on what you would like your wealth to achieve for you and your family. Otherwise, your long-term planning can get derailed by reacting to the daily stream of information that bombards you.

The Wealth Cycle

Too many wealthy families fall prey to the Wealth Cycle. That is especially true of those who define wealth in narrow financial terms. If you understand the three types of capital—financial, social and human—you can skirt the common pitfalls of wealthy families in your financial, legal and life planning.

Variations on the phrase "Shirtsleeves to shirtsleeves in three generations" occur around the world. In the U.S., it dates back to the late 1800s, the time of men like J.P. Morgan and the Vanderbilts, entrepreneurs who left behind companies or flashy estates that survive today.

The Wealth Cycle begins with the entrepreneurial creator of the wealth who works hard, accumulates financial capital, and lives below his means. Working in shirtsleeves refers to working in a hands-on capacity, often in industries or occupations that are low status or offer uncertain rewards.

The creator of wealth then passes that hard-earned financial wealth to his children. They attend the best universities (in contrast with the wealth creator, who may have had a very poor formal education), wear designer styles, and live in relative splendor.

Next, the wealth creator's children pass wealth on to their children, the third generation. This generation knows nothing but living with wealth. They may not be disposed to hard work, but are often adept at spending money. Often, they run through the family's capital. As a result, many children of the fourth generation return in shirtsleeves to the common labor force.

Most wealth creators would prefer that their family avoid the Shirtsleeves Cycle, but they don't know how to make that happen. We have learned from our work with wealthy families that you need to plan for the three types of capital in order to avoid the Shirtsleeves Cycle.

Start by thinking about what wealth means to you in the broadest possible terms. Ask yourself the following questions:

- What constitutes wealth?
- What is wealth good for?
- What are the dangers of wealth?
- What opportunities does wealth represent?
- What strengths can be reinforced by wealth?

If you need help getting started, review these quotes about wealth.

CHAPTER FOUR

Wealth is the organized capacity of society to apply generalized principles toward present and future life support.
—Buckminster Fuller, Operating Manual for Spaceship Earth

Wealth is your total assets minus your total liabilities.
—Your accountants

Wealth is evidently not the good we are seeking; for it is merely useful for the sake of something else.
—Aristotle, Nicomachean Ethics

Wealth is friends, home, father, brother, title to respect and fame. Yes, wealth is confused for wisdom—that it should be so is shame."
—The Book of Good Counsels, a Sanskrit text, ca. 300 B.C.

All wealth is power, so power must infallibly draw wealth to itself by some means or other.
—Edmund Burke, in an observation made to the House of Commons in the eighteenth century

Money ranks with love as man's greatest joy. And it ranks with death as his greatest source of anxiety.
—John Kenneth Galbraith, The Age of Uncertainty

Of all forms of tyranny the least attractive and the most vulgar is the tyranny of wealth; the tyranny of plutocracy.
—J. Pierpont Morgan's autobiography

In summary, wealth has been described as the **capacity** to take action, as **relationships**, as the root of both **luxury** and **indolence**, and as a **tyrant**. It has also been described as the **value of people**—human capital—the knowledge, skills, values, attitudes, and wisdom of members of a family (and other people important to the family) certainly constitute wealth.

Now that you understand that wealth must be defined broadly, it is time to consider the types of capital that comprise wealth.

The Three Types of Capital

There are three types of capital:

- **Financial Capital**—what you own
- **Social Capital**—how you and your family relate to society, your philanthropies, your taxes paid to support the common good, volunteering of your time and talents
- **Human Capital**—the people important to your family and family systems, your skills, knowledge, values, intellectual capital, and stories

Most family leaders focus on planning their financial capital. They fail to give equal attention to growing their human or social capital. However, other family members care differently and to varying degrees about the three types of capital, potentially creating friction. In the end, all types of capital are interrelated and important.

The main decision-makers about the family's financial capital must consider the members of the family who are supported by "the money," or who define themselves in terms of "the money."

For those in the family who are most passionate about charities and social causes, financial capital is the instrument for achieving desired good works. Other family members may be unable to relate to this type of passion, so they criticize it as a way to enhance and extend the "do-gooder's" personal influence.

Social capital is often difficult to plan for, as there may not be a central focus for philanthropy among all the members of the family. If this is the situation, you may want to provide the flexibility of individualized philanthropic plans.

The family founder, whose intellectual capital and hard work created the family fortune, often wishes to preserve the family's skills, wisdom, and personal values. This desire can create problems, especially if the entrepreneur who started the business is ill-suited to transition the company into a long-term operating mode.

Thinking about Financial Capital

Financial capital, for most people, is the easiest of the three forms of wealth to understand. It is measured in units of currency. It includes stocks, bonds, and real estate as well as instruments derived from them, such as mutual funds, hedge funds, venture funds, certificates of ownership, forward-selling contracts, stock options, private equity holdings and other forms of financial interest.

The generation that first develops great financial capital usually does so by converting **intellectual property** (a great idea or invention that you use) into **intellectual capital** (an idea or invention that others buy and use). This conversion requires hard work, personal and family sacrifice and, more often than not, results in a number of setbacks and failures before the "overnight success" occurs.

Sometimes the accumulation of capital starts slowly and builds up over time, allowing the accumulators to develop skill at handling their finances. In other situations, big money appears suddenly, such as with the sale of the business, directly or through a public offering of ownership, or through stock options.

"Sudden money" events mean that the recipients do not have time to prepare psychologically or technically for their financial windfall.[4] The Integrated Planning Process provides a useful structure for such individuals.

Thinking about Social Capital

We define social capital as "a family's impact on society through its philanthropy." Boston-based planner Scott Fithian[5] encourages families to refocus their thinking about their legacy by shifting the emphasis "from success to significance."

Society has mandated each person's support of the common good through a governmental system of taxation. Funds are collected by local, state, and federal governments to provide services and structures for the public. If you do nothing in terms of planning for your social capital, you are still destined to be an **involuntary philanthropist** through your taxes. Fortunately, the tax code also allows you to organize your affairs in order to redirect some or all of this would-be tax money directly to approved charities.

The government encourages direct philanthropy because it is a more efficient channel for supplying social services. A new charity applies to the federal government for a tax-free designation that permits people to make contributions directly to the charity and then take a charitable deduction when calculating their personal taxes. Direct contributions cut out the middleman (agencies of the state and federal government) and the cost of the middleman's bureaucracy.

By encouraging **voluntary philanthropy** to organizations described in section 501(c)(3) and other sections of the Internal Revenue Code, the government gains the help of people who can quickly

---

[4] Susan Bradley's *Sudden Money*™: *Managing a Financial Windfall* (New York: John Wiley & Sons, Inc., 2000) focuses on this topic.

[5] Scott C. Fithian is recognized throughout the US and Canada as a pioneer in the tools and methodology of Values-Based Planning™.

identify emerging issues and provide funds to agencies who will deal with those issues.

You and your family will have choices as you consider how to accomplish your philanthropic goals. For example, as attorney Patricia Annino has observed, "There are many types of charitable giving vehicles to consider: charitable bequests, life insurance, gift annuities, pooled income funds, charitable remainder trusts, charitable lead trusts, donor advised funds and private foundations."[6] Your team can assist you in selecting the most appropriate options.

Social capital also involves hands-on work with charities and agencies. By serving on charitable boards, you leave a legacy to society. That work can also help other family members understand your family's objectives and values and learn skills related to working with other people with similar visions and values.

Many families use activities related to their chosen charities and philanthropic endeavors to teach children and grandchildren about tax laws, money management, and group governance. Some families who have private foundations or supporting organizations create advisory board positions for adult children and grandchildren to begin their wealth training. By demonstrating the importance of giving and becoming involved in important emerging issues in our society, you can greatly influence the hearts and minds of your heirs.

Thinking about Human Capital

Your family's human capital consists of the knowledge, skills, attitudes, values, and wisdom of your family members and the people important to you. It is also the informal family systems and the more formalized governance protocols that families sometimes create to manage decision-making and relationships.

---

[6] Patricia Annino, *Women & Money: A Practical Guide to Estate Planning* (BookSurge Publishing, 2004). Patricia Annino is a nationally recognized authority on estate planning and regularly assists high net worth families.

This capital may be the most valuable to the family and at the same time the most difficult to transmit from generation to generation. People too often overestimate the extent to which the family's human capital is understood by their family members. Therefore, it is important to be very clear about what you want for yourself and your heirs.

Aging parents and their adult children may look at the same challenge or experience from perspectives that seem 180 degrees apart, according to authors John W. Gibson and Bonnie Brown Hartley in their book *The Dynamics of Aging Families*.

More than 70 percent of high net worth families said their estate plans failed to achieve their family's goals, in a survey of more than 3,000 families conducted by the Williams Group.[7] The study team tried to identify why there was such a high rate of perceived failure. Only about three percent failed due to either faulty planning or tax code provisions that frustrated their plans. Rather, they discovered that while the parents thought their children understood their parents' goals, objectives and values, the children said they had "hardly a clue!"

This generational disconnect was one of the principal reasons for the failure of a family's estate plan. What is the lesson for you? When you provide training in the skills, competencies, and experience for managing financial, social, and human capital, you lay the foundation for your children and grandchildren to become good stewards of wealth rather than dissipaters of wealth.

Knowing when and how to involve an heir in family plans is important to the long-term success of your financial and legal plan. In *Preparing Heirs*, Willams and Presser encourage family leaders to focus on training each heir.

The lack of a clearly articulated and cohesive financial strategy, combined with an inadequate strategy for maximizing the human potential of each member of the family, arguably the greatest store-

---

[7] The Williams Group, headed by Roy Williams and Vic Presser, is a financial planning organization based in Colorado. Messrs. Williams and Presser are the authors of *Preparing Heirs*.

house of value within the family, causes many of the problems that face the family.

Accordingly, make sure your integrated financial and legal plan considers all three forms of capital. Starting with the Evaluation Stage, the *Integrated Planning Process* will guide you to achieve this.

KEY CONCEPTS

- A thoughtful plan that prepares your heirs and beneficiaries for their wealth and their part in the family's strategies is crucial if they are to enjoy the benefits—and minimize the burdens—of family wealth.

- Make sure that your integrated financial and legal plan considers all three forms of wealth: financial (what you own), social (your family's impact on society through its philanthropy) and human (your family's skills, knowledge and values which are also embodied in informal family systems).

- Involve your children in your family systems and decision-making to help them understand your family's human capital.

Chapter Five

Integrated Planning Process™ Pre-Engagement Stage Stage 1 – Evaluation

Now that you understand the three types of capital, you can continue your journey through the *Integrated Planning Process*.

The *Integrated Planning Process* is comparable to building a house. You begin with the architecture—the high-level conceptual ideal. That equates to the *Evaluation* and *Goals Development* stages. The *Plan Design*, *Implementation* and *Plan Oversight and Governance* stages involve "architectural," "construction," and "maintenance" activities.

One of the most important parts of the *Evaluation* and the *Goals Development* stages is personal chemistry. It does not relate directly to your financial and legal situation. Yet without it, your plan may fail.

All of the parties to your *Integrated Planning Process* must have relationships with good chemistry. You may say, "But I already know my financial planner and my attorney. What's the big deal about adding a few more parties and getting them to cooperate?"

The Tone of the Relationship (Chemistry)

For a planning process that both your family and your team deem successful, all parties must be able to work well together. You and your family must develop a deep trust in your team as a whole, in addition to individually. Similarly, your team members will perform best when they enjoy working with you, your family and each other. An ongoing harmonious working relationship, based on mutual respect and trust with the potential to grow over time, is essential.

"Clients for life" and "Work should be fun" are two expressions that summarize our approach to professional relationships. "Clients for life" means that we expect to have our clients for the rest of our professional lives so we had better really like each other. Clients become professional friends, and we expect those friendships to last.

"Work should be fun" reflects our philosophy that life is too short to do things that are not fun—for you and for us. Besides, if the process is fun, we all do a better job!

Pre-Engagement Stage – Getting Acquainted

It is important for you and your team to get acquainted before you begin the five stages of integrated planning. This lays the groundwork for all of you working together comfortably and efficiently.

A two- to four-hour meeting to discuss "big picture" issues is the key component of this *Pre-Engagement Stage*. You will tell the team about the key characteristics of your family situation. In turn, you will receive information about the benefits and requirements of the *Integrated Planning Process*.

This period of open conversation will set expectations for you, your family and your team. It will also ensure that you understand the process and that you and your team members feel confident about your decision to proceed.

During the *Evaluation* and *Goals Development* stages that follow, you and your team get to test the chemistry that developed during the *Pre-Engagement Stage*. It is a two-way street. In our experience, good chemistry comes from a healthy mixture of humor, pleasant personalities and mutual respect. It also helps for each of the parties to have a cooperative spirit, punctuality, reliability, openness, philanthropic nature, thoughtfulness, decisiveness, and willingness to be a good team player.

Stage 1 – Evaluation

In the *Evaluation Stage*, your team will collect information so they can understand your starting point. This information will become part of the foundation of your integrated plan.

The *Evaluation Stage* is not an exhaustive study of your situation—that happens in the *Plan Design Stage*—instead, it is an overview that will enable your team to understand your general situation and decide if they can provide you with the service you need.

You may find it helpful to think of your team's questions as analogous to the questions that an architect would ask you before designing your new home. An architect would ask about your house's location, rooms, garage requirements, and other amenities.

In other words, the architect would need to know your basic requirements, desires and budget. The same goes for the members of your integrated financial and legal planning team. We have listed some sample questions in the box.

Retirement
- How much financial capital do you expect to accumulate before retirement?
- When do you expect to retire?
- Do you need a business succession plan?

Financial help for family members
- Do you plan to pay for grandchildren's education?
- Do you plan to help your children start a new business or continue in your business?
- Do you plan to support the financial need of parents or other family members?

Planned expenditures
- Additional homes?
- Boats?
- Planes?

Philanthropy
- What are your plans for charitable giving?
- Will you create a family foundation?

Your legacy
- What are the plans for informing your children about your plan and wishes?
- How do you want to be remembered?

Your team cannot assess the potential for realizing your desires without collecting basic information about your current financial, legal and family situation using the documents listed in the box that follows.

The documents necessary for a basic overview of your family's situation include:

☐ Last three years of income tax returns

☐ Your personal balance sheet (in other words, a list of your assets and liabilities)

☐ Financial statements for family-owned business, if applicable

☐ All estate planning documents

☐ Copies of all life insurance policies including beneficiary designations

☐ Business agreements, including those regarding:
- Stock redemption
- Buy-sell for business interests
- Employment contracts

☐ Statements for:
- Investment accounts
- Retirement plans, including beneficiary designations

☐ Detailed information regarding personal and business liabilities

☐ Other documents and agreements relevant to the topics discussed above

Once you and your team believe that the team understands your situation, the team should evaluate its capacity to be valuable and helpful to you and your family. The report of that evaluation and your response to it will govern whether or not you and the team proceed to the *Goals Development Stage*.

For example, if the team believes that it can be beneficial, and you and the team feel your chemistry works, then you would proceed. If the details of your situation or the chemistry are not a good fit for you or your team, then you would look elsewhere for a team.

Key Concepts

- Good chemistry among team members is essential for success. The chemistry will be tested during the *Evaluation Stage*.

- Your journey begins with collecting information about your present circumstances. You cannot progress unless you know where you are now and where you want to go in the future.

Chapter Six

Integrated Planning Process™ Stage 2 – Goals Development

The Importance of Goals Development

You may think, "I just want a plan, I do not want the inconvenience of this goals setting stuff." Think again.

As the old adage says, "As you climb the ladder of success be sure it is leaning on the correct wall."

Without a clearly defined set of family goals your professional advisers are just guessing about the shape of your plan. That can lead to "garbage in, garbage out," in the words of the computer industry.

If you spend money on an integrated plan, you should also invest time to ensure that it is based on correct, complete information, so it can accomplish your true goals.

The first step to attaining your goals is to have a family vision/goals statement as a starting point for providing direction, confidence and capability for the members of your family. It is important to do this correctly, or you could get sidetracked.

The Sub-Goal Trap

Most families like yours have not clearly established their overall life goals in personal or financial terms. Perhaps you have set individual goals with each adviser in their specialty area. The problem with this sub-goal approach is that you never focus on where you really want to go. We call this The Sub-Goal Trap.

As a result of focusing on sub-goals at the expense of the big picture, you may:

- Make individual and isolated decisions that are conflicting and not mutually supportive
- Waste time and lose money pursuing the wrong sub-goals
- Fail to achieve your overall life goals

Vision vs. Goals

Another trap that you may encounter is failing to distinguish between your family's vision and your goals. It is essential for your team to understand both your vision and your goals.

Your vision is a broad direction in which you would like to head. When your team understands your vision, they can make valuable, big picture inferences about your family. Goals are more concrete and shorter-term.

Here are three examples that demonstrate the difference between a vision and a goal.

Vision	Goal
Travel extensively	Spend a month in a different country each year
Support charitable organizations	Make a gift of $500,000 to local hospital capital campaign Serve as a member of a board of directors for a local private school
Support the development of the grandchildren	Vacation/travel one week per year with each grandchild Pay for grandchildren's educations

Now that you understand the importance of goals and the difference between your vision and your goals, you are ready to begin the goal-setting process. In the next chapter, we will walk you through two case studies.

Key Concepts

- If you lack clearly defined personal and financial goals, you may waste time and money pursuing the wrong sub-goals.

- You and your team should create a broad vision for your family, along with specific goals, before you advance further in creating your integrated financial and legal plan.

Chapter Seven
Integrated Planning Process™ Goals Development Case Study

You can begin the goal-setting process in partnership with the lead members of your team. The best way to develop and identify goals is for the family leaders to meet with their lead advisers in a setting isolated from distractions. This meeting may last from two hours to two days, depending upon the complexity of your financial and personal circumstances. Your advisers will serve as your coaches, helping you develop your vision and goals.

Now it is time to introduce you to our two case study families—the Youngs and the Retireds. Mr. and Mrs. Young are a composite of clients with young families, while Mr. and Mrs. Retired represent some priorities typical of families with grown children.

The Young Family

Mr. and Mrs. Young are both age 40 and in good health. They both have professional graduate degrees and stable professional jobs with combined annual salaries of $245,000.

They have two children, a boy age 14 and a girl age 17. Their daughter is preparing for college and wants to attend an Ivy League school. Their son is involved in the Boy Scouts and is interested in oceanography.

Mrs. Young's parents own a manufacturing firm, so Mrs. Young stands to inherit shares in the family business worth more than $10 million. Her parents have already set up a trust for her and her siblings, which holds company stock currently valued at $5 million. It yields $100,000 in annual pre-tax income for the Youngs.

Mr. Young's parents are comfortable financially, but his mother's health is deteriorating. Medical bills may eventually deplete what his parents have accumulated. Mr. Young's financial position is the strongest of his siblings, so it may fall to him to support his parents in later years.

The Retired Family

Mr. and Mrs. Retired's circumstances differ significantly from those of the Young family, partly because of their age. Mr. Retired is age 72 and his wife is age 70. They are both in good health and enjoy traveling.

The Retireds have four children: a son, 52, who runs the family business; a son, 50, who is permanently disabled and estranged from his older brother; a daughter, 48, who is an attorney; and a son, 41, who is working on his Ph.D. in archeology.

They have three grandchildren by two of their children: a grandson, 27, who just graduated from business school and recently married; a granddaughter, 23, in a graduate fine arts program; and a granddaughter, 18, getting ready to enter college. Their other two children are unmarried and childless.

Mr. and Mrs. Retired receive $1 million annually in dividends from their interest in the family business, currently valued at $25 million. They have $5 million in investment accounts and $1 million in retirement accounts.

The Retireds are philanthropically minded, so they would like to develop a plan to support their favorite causes more effectively and expansively. They are concerned about the fractured relationship between their two oldest sons, but do not know what to do about it. They are very interested in helping their grandchildren obtain high quality educations.

Questions that Can Uncover Your Vision and Goals

Despite their very different situations, the Young and Retired families need to consider a similar set of questions. We believe it is important to ask the right questions because "The quality of your questions determines the quality of your life."[8]

Here are some of the questions you should consider:

- Are you doing what you like to do—and delegating what you don't like to do?
- What are your long-term and short-term financial goals for yourselves, your children and your parents?
- Which philanthropies do you wish to support, and how can you balance your charitable contributions and resources?
- How can you pass your values and traditions (human capital) to your children and grandchildren?
- What will happen to your family home when you die?
- What are the legal and financial options that will help you achieve your goals?
- Who can you turn to for help?

Your team can customize these questions to your personal situation to speed your goal-setting process.

---

[8]Byron E. Woodman, III, is founder of *QuestionsForLiving*®, an organization committed to helping people learn the questions which will improve their decision-making and help them achieve better results.

When we asked Mr. and Mrs. Young what they **love to do** in various aspects of their life, this is how they answered.

Life Aspect	Loves To Do
Family	Spend time with our children, participating in their interests and education
Recreation	Play tennis, ride horses, rock climb
Professional Development	Participate in business and professional activities that add meaning to our lives
Financial	Be self-supporting, provide educational advantages to children, care for Mr. Young's parents if needed
Spirituality	Have time to grow spiritually and support our faith's religious institutions
Philanthropy	Support our church, the Boy Scouts and the Oceanographic Institute
Legal Matters and Estate Planning	Have peace of mind that our estate and asset protection plans are in place and will accomplish our family's goals over the long term

We also asked Mr. and Mrs. Young what they **do not like to do and what they prefer to delegate**. They replied that they do not like to:

- Continually watch and worry over our finances
- Take sole responsibility for investment decisions to ensure sufficient cash flow to take care of our children's futures, Mr. Young's parents, and our lifestyle
- Budget and pay bills
- Spend time doing repetitive household tasks

Turning to Mr. and Mrs. Retired, we see a different set of priorities in what they **love to do**.

Life Aspect	Loves To Do
Family	Spend time with children and grandchildren, helping them learn about interesting things like art, music, sports, spirituality and travel
Recreation	Traveling, golfing, sailing, playing bridge
Professional Development	Mentor our children and key business associates
Financial	Be good stewards of our financial capital and the family business
Spirituality	Support the mission of our church worldwide
Philanthropy	Support our local place of worship, the art museum and children's issues
Legal Matters and Estate Planning	Have peace of mind that our estate and asset protection plans are in place and will accomplish our family's goals over the long term, develop a plan to pass ownership of the family business to the next generation

Mr. and Mrs. Retired were also clear about what they **do not like to do**:

- Take on any commitments that do not add meaning to our lives
- Spend time watching over financial or legal matters that can be taken care of by others
- Pay bills
- Spend time on property maintenance
- Worry about the uncertainties and complexity of financial, legal and business succession matters

The Youngs' and the Retireds' comprehensive list of questions led them to a clear understanding of what adds meaning to their lives. For some families, answering these questions will ready them to begin the planning stage of the process. Others will want to probe further.

Two Strategic Tools

Two strategic tools provide the intellectual underpinnings of the questions we asked the Youngs and the Retireds during their goal-setting process. One is the R-Factor Question®. The second is the D.O.S. (Dangers Opportunities and Strengths) analysis that is similar to the corporate Strengths, Weaknesses, Opportunities, and Threats (SWOT) exercise.[9]

The R-Factor Question might more aptly be called the Success Question for our purposes. It is: If we were looking back to today three years from now, what has to have happened in that period of time for you to be happy with your progress personally and professionally?

The answer to this question provides a wealth of information about your desired direction in life, what constitutes success to you, and what is your definition of happiness.

The D.O.S. analysis keeps your family management system focused on what is most important to your family members. It keeps a portion of your team's attention trained on your future and the **dangers** to be avoided, the **opportunities** to be captured, and the **strengths** to be developed and reinforced in your family.

Because this information is so important, we ask about it not only during the *Goals Development Stage*, but also during the *Evaluation* and *Plan Oversight and Governance* stages. It helps us to ensure that your plan adapts to your changing circumstances.

---

[9]The R-Factor Question® and The D.O.S. Conversation™ are integral concepts, trademarks, and protected copyrights of The Strategic Coach, Inc. All rights reserved. Used with written permission. www.strategiccoach.com The Strategic Coach Program™, a life focusing program for successful entrepreneurs, was developed by Dan Sullivan, President and Co-Founder of The Strategic Coach, Inc.

For examples of dangers, opportunities, and strengths, read the exhibit below. You can use it as a checklist. The section on *Thinking Strategically*, which follows, illustrates how dangers, opportunities and strengths may translate into goals.

Examples of Dangers, Opportunities and Strengths

Frequently Overlooked Dangers	Income taxes Lack of integrated financial and legal plan Lack of training on how to deal with inheritance Too much money too soon
Commonly Noticed Dangers	Creditors Disability Divorce Exposure to estate taxes Feeling overwhelmed by the complexity of wealth Loss of: confidence, control, relationships, reputation, time, time value of money Litigation
Frequently Overlooked Opportunities	Creation of team to monitor and manage estate and financial plans Creation of an integrated financial and legal plan Passing wisdom to future generations Venture philanthropy
Commonly Noticed Opportunities	Delegating activities to professional advisers Direct investment into small businesses Encouraging children to pursue their unique abilities regardless of economic consequences Mentoring junior family members and business associates Philanthropy and volunteering as a way to have an impact on society Real estate speculation Tax savings Use time as you wish Working with a professional advisory team
Frequently Overlooked Strengths	Capacity for contingency planning
Commonly Noticed Strengths	Capacity to: communicate, make decisions, receive and evaluate advice, think strategically Commitment to community Enthusiasm for life Health and vitality Mentor/mentee opportunities Opportunities for formal and informal education of children Wisdom

Thinking Strategically

The family needs to be able to think about the **dangers** that face them and how to avoid or mitigate those dangers. For example, the Retired family's financial capital is based on an operating company that was founded by the family's patriarch, Robert Retired. Unless proper steps are taken to prepare for the death of Robert, the company may be forced into liquidation or sale to outside investors when funds are required to pay estate taxes.[10]

Robert's eldest son, currently the chief operating officer but only a minority shareholder, is in danger of being displaced by new management, if a sale were to occur. This causes the son anxiety and affects his quality of life, but he feels he is in no position to encourage defensive actions. This danger to the family's finances and human capital should be recognized and strategies should be developed to avoid unpleasant outcomes.

Family members need to be able to recognize and think about the **opportunities** that are available to them and the ways to take advantage of those opportunities. For example, the Young family has a son showing an interest in oceanography. There is an oceanographic institute on the coast nearby the Young's home. Mr. and Mrs. Young have been searching for ways to act on their philanthropic impulses and support of the institute could both satisfy their philanthropic desires and create opportunities for their son to more fully explore his interests.

The **strengths** of the family as a whole and of individual members in the family can be developed and reinforced. For example, Robert and Karen Retired have a daughter just entering the legal profession. By involving her on the family advisory board, they can at once involve her more fully in their family's vision for the future and expose her to sophisticated financial and legal planning strategies and the various consultants and disciplines involved in the family governance.

---

[10] An excellent resource on succession planning is Bonnie Brown Hartley's *Sudden Death: A Fire Drill for Building Strength and Flexibility in Families* (Venice, FL.: Cambio Press, 2005). Her book reflects her experience as a facilitator of succession and contingency planning.

The family needs to understand the rules of brainstorming, a useful tool for thinking strategically. The best ideas are not always the first ideas, but they may evolve from the first "crazy" or "impractical" ideas. Try not to let anticipated difficulties in implementing one of these first ideas impede the brainstorming process. During these brainstorming sessions, you should focus on:

- Asking questions
- Exploring possibilities
- Identifying the types of information needed
- Locating information sources

The views of the oldest generation often carry the greatest weight, particularly if that generation's intellectual capital and hard work produced the family's financial capital. They may be so powerful that other members of the family participating in the thinking process decline to fully participate. If this is likely to be the case, it may be wise to include outside consultants[11] to assure that everyone's best thinking is represented.

Once you have adopted a written statement of your goals, you are ready to advance to the *Plan Design Stage*. It is important to know that your goals will not be set in stone; over time you will be able to revise them as you see your circumstances unfold. Your life goals are not just financial goals; they encompass all aspects of your vision for you, your family, and your life.

---

[11] There are different types of consultants who may meet your needs, depending on your specific circumstances. Some possibilities include facilitators of succession planning, psychologists, coaches and professional mediators.

Key Concepts

- Asking the right questions will help you identify meaningful goals for you and your family.

- Consider what you and your family members love to do as well as your family's dangers, opportunities and strengths.

- Involve as many family members as is appropriate in setting your goals.

Chapter Eight
Integrated Planning Process™
Stage 3 – Plan Design
Stage 4 – Implementation

To continue the house-building analogy, once your goals have been established, it is time for the architect and the contractor to develop a blueprint. This happens in the *Plan Design Stage*. Next, construction begins with the *Implementation Stage*. Monitoring and maintenance follows in the *Plan Oversight and Governance Stage*.

During the *Plan Design Stage* you develop your family's long-term plan for getting the right capital to the right people at the right time.

It's important to think long-term. Some experts, such as attorney James E. Hughes, believe you should make a 100-year plan for success.[12] If you do not plan that far in advance, your wealth may well disappear in three generations, says Hughes. If that is daunting, consider a 25-year plan. The important thing is to prepare your family to grow and prosper in the long run.

---

[12] James E. Hughes, Jr., *Family Wealth—Keeping it in the Family: How Family Members and Their Advisers Preserve Human, Intellectual, and Financial Assets for Generations* (Bloomberg Press, 2004).

During the *Plan Design Stage*, your team should:

- Take a "Big Picture" or holistic approach to ensure that your strategies are compatible and support your vision of the future
- Develop a thorough and detailed plan (the blueprint)
- Educate you about the design, so you can ask questions, participate in design refinements and ultimately adopt the design with confidence that it will accomplish your goals

Let's look at each of these points in more detail.

Take a Holistic Approach

Your team should use "big picture" thinking. To tailor your financial and legal system to your unique goals, your team must consider many factors, including, for example, your ages, health, assets, other family members and their skills, capacities, and needs, and your existing financial and legal plan.

Remember, this is not exclusively a plan for your financial assets. The design team should consider integrated strategies for transferring each of your family's three forms of wealth in accordance with the goals you established. The team then should create a design that is composed of as many financial and legal solutions as needed for your family's unique circumstances.

Developing Your Detailed Plan

You may see a comprehensive picture of your financial situation for the first time, as your team does its job. A thorough and detailed plan should begin with the preparation of your balance sheet, complete with footnotes explaining every asset and liability. To develop this, the team should start with the information gained during the *Evaluation Stage*, and then the team should work closely with your CPA, investment advisers, insurance advisers, attorneys and the human resource departments that can provide information regarding your corporate benefit programs.

When the design team has the facts—financial and legal—and knowledge of your goals and family dynamics, they can develop ideas on how to structure your plan. The team applies the diversified experience of its members to refine and develop a draft of your plan.

Your team will use sophisticated tools for plan development. For example, computer models may be used to simulate the cash flows from the various elements of the design to make sure that they fulfill your family's expectations for its lifestyle and legacy to both heirs and charities. The cash flow and tax characteristics of each of the new entities, integrated with your existing entities, are used to craft optimal portfolios for each entity, as well as an overarching Investment Policy Statement for your family's financial wealth.

Your Participation

You should understand the plan so that you can evaluate its appropriateness for you and your family. Also, you should have the opportunity to suggest modifications so that the plan more closely matches your wishes. This is an evolutionary process, so your team expects and welcomes your input.

The following process has worked well for our clients. We suggest this as a basis for the approach used by you and your team.

1. **Your team provides you with the plan as a series of "solutions" compiled into a loose leaf binder.** The solutions may be shown in three ways—in written text, numerically, and in charts, so that the information is easily accessible by people with differing learning styles. Also, there may be summaries that clearly illustrate the "bottom line." Usually, more detailed explanations are presented in case you want to look "under the hood."

2. **You have a meeting with the team.** Make sure there is ample time for the plan to be presented and explained to you. During that meeting, your questions and concerns will be addressed.

3. **You review the plan after the presentation meeting.** This may spur additional questions and comments. As needed, you will have follow-up discussions with team members.

4. **Your team provides an implementation checklist.** It shows who will be involved in the implementation, what their responsibilities will be, and when specific tasks should be completed.

Once you have completed this process, it is time to move to the *Implementation Stage*.

Stage 4 – Implementation
"The devil is in the details."

The implementation checklist described above is the key to the *Implementation Stage*. Here is an example of a section of an implementation checklist for a design solution that establishes a qualified supporting organization.

Action Items	Responsible Party	Target Date	Completion Date
Draft Supporting Organization (SO) Trust	Law Firm		
Draft SO Policy Statement	Accountant or Law Firm		
Apply for Tax Exempt Status	Law Firm		
Set up account	Family Board		
Transfer Assets	Family Board		
Draft Letter Agreements for SO and obtain IRS determination letters	Law Firm		
Manage SO	Trustees and Family Board		
Prepare Annual Tax and Information Returns	Family Board		

It is important that your team work closely together to implement every detail of the plan. The implementation must be done accurately and thoroughly or the design will not work as intended. Your team should accept the responsibility for all of the details involved with the implementation of your plan.

By the time you and your team have finished the *Implementation Stage*, you have accomplished the most labor-intensive stage of the process. However, the beauty of an integrated plan is that it is not static. It evolves as your circumstances change. This occurs during the *Plan Oversight and Governance Stage*.

KEY CONCEPTS

- The main goal of plan design is to get the right capital to the right family members at the right time.

- Your plan design process should culminate in a book of "solutions" that will be presented to you in person. You should review and give feedback on the plan after the meeting, so it can be revised as necessary.

- Your implementation checklist will describe which team members are responsible for achieving which tasks by what time. It ensures that your decisions are implemented accurately and on time.

Chapter Nine

Integrated Planning Process™ Stage 5 – Plan Oversight and Governance

Plan Oversight and Governance gives you peace of mind. Your Family Board, composed of key family and professional team members, is essential to this process. It generally incorporates the people involved in the Integrated Planning Process.

Your Role and Your Family's Role in Stage 5

The professionals on your Family Board will manage your financial and legal plan, so you don't have to worry about a long "To do" list of financial and legal items. They make it easy for you to achieve the results you want from your plan.

Your relationship with your new integrated financial and legal plan should be similar to your relationship with your car. Most people want to simply turn the key in the ignition and have their car work. They do not want to dig into the automobile's innards. If your team is on the ball, your plan should run as smoothly as a finely tuned, well-maintained automobile.

Your input will be small, but very important. We use the following graphic to show the interface.

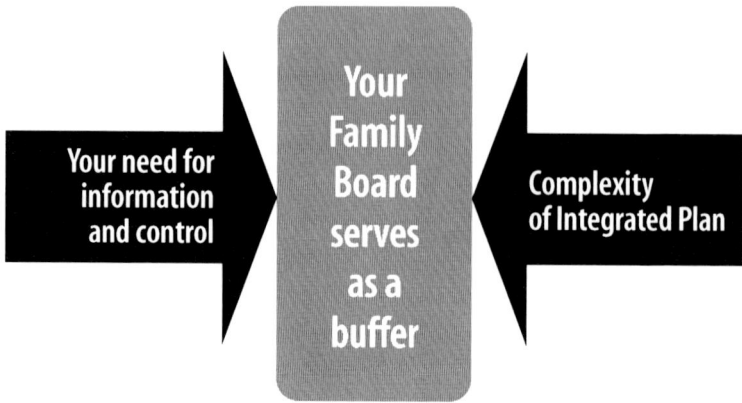

Once your integrated plan is implemented, most of the team's time will be devoted to helping you make better—and more strategic—decisions.

Your team will want to develop excellent communication among the family members and the lead advisers who serve on the Family Board as well as outside advisers who are called upon to serve occasionally, such as valuation experts.

Take the time to communicate with your team about your information needs. Tell them what type of information you require, how detailed communications should be, the form they should take, and the frequency with which they should be delivered.

Good communication includes the use of meeting agendas and the preparation of meeting minutes. These tools keep the members of the Family Board literally and figuratively on the same page, at the same time. They create confidence within your family that it has chosen a good direction and is progressing towards its objectives.

You may wish to involve family members other than yourself, so you can prepare them to assume roles of responsibility on behalf of the family. This may include participation on the Family Board or managing special projects for the family.

You will want to establish clear criteria for adding a family member to the Family Board. These criteria should include consideration of the personal interests, skills, and competencies needed for effective family governance and continuity. Serving on the Family Board and assisting with special projects can be an effective training ground for heirs.

For example, if it made sense for the Retired family to have a conservation easement placed on a property, their attorney daughter might take responsibility for working with professionals and governmental agencies to establish the easement. The Retired family would benefit from the easement; the daughter would benefit from gaining a new experience.

Your Team's Role

Now let us examine your team's role during Stage 5. Your team should take control of the complex details of administering your plan. They should ensure that all the systems and strategies are functioning properly. By this we mean that the team coordinates such things as insurance coverage, tax compliance, and facilitating payments.

A good plan is not static. It should adapt to changes. Your team should help you stay alert for dangers to be avoided or mitigated, and opportunities to be captured. These dangers and opportunities can arise from changes outside of your family, such as:

- Investment market conditions
- Tax laws
- Political circumstances
- Laws generally, such as those that govern creditor rights and health care

They could also reflect changes within your family, such as:

- Marriages
- Births
- Retirement
- Deaths
- Divorces
- New business ventures
- New philanthropic commitments

The ways that your team helps you adapt include financial and legal research, philanthropic planning, and the thoughtful preparation of your heirs. In fact, the preparation of the next generation may be one of the most important functions of your team. Developing informational sessions for your heirs can help ensure that your family members are prepared for the benefits and burdens of wealth.

Helpful Processes

You and your team will probably establish internal controls to buffer yourself from the complexity of your integrated financial and legal plan. You will delegate a number of the management and monitoring responsibilities to the members of the team. The team will design, with your input, a customized information system to maintain your confidence as it supplies you with information and control capabilities.

It is in the best interest of everyone involved in your organization system to have a carefully documented set of policies, procedures, and processes. Flowcharts may be used to show how each process is performed, controlled, and monitored.

Once the processes are fully documented, a set of internal controls is identified. Every member of the team should be fully aware of the processes that he or she is responsible for and for the ways to amend those processes. While the team leader has ultimate responsibility for this process, he or she should receive the wholehearted support of the team members.

You may wish to engage an independent firm to conduct periodic examinations of the documents and reflect on the actions taken. This will help ensure that each member performs his or her assigned process in an appropriate manner and that all transactions are properly documented. These steps will provide the accountability required for managing and monitoring the complex systems that have been established to achieve the long-term benefits of your integrated financial and legal plan.

Judging Your Plan's Effectiveness

In our experience, happy clients have a lot in common. They feel that their team provides them with the information they need to make decisions, feel in control, and have peace of mind. At the same time, they are not overburdened with petty details because the team effectively manages those for them.

Our Plan Effectiveness Checklist (see box) lists the components of a satisfied client's typical plan. You may not need every element because your plan will be tailored to your unique circumstances. However, if you are missing one of these components, you may wish to discuss it with your team.

Plan Effectiveness Checklist

Do you and your family have:

☐ Written goals against which you can measure your progress

☐ An integrated financial and legal plan

☐ A plan for financial capital with benchmarks to measure performance

☐ A plan for social capital which your children understand and participate in

☐ A plan for human capital, so your family is committed to lifelong learning

☐ A team that effectively buffers you from the complexity of your administrative issues, such as tax compliance and portfolio rebalancing.

The *Plan Oversight and Governance Stage* is not glamorous, but it is essential to your peace of mind. You can sleep soundly once you have put in place the processes of Stage 5.

Key Concepts

- Plan oversight and governance by your team will help buffer you from the complexity of your integrated financial, legal and life plan because it allows you to delegate much of your administrative work to your team. It also ensures that your plan changes as your circumstances change.

- During this phase, your team focuses on helping you to make better, more strategic decisions that will further your pursuit of your goals.

- Communication—between you and your team and with other family members—is essential to the success of your plan. It also helps family members to understand the overall family goals and prepares them for broader responsibilities in the future.

- This phase should include a system of internal controls over the various processes managed by your team. You may also wish to have compliance with your system of internal controls verified periodically by an independent firm.

Chapter Ten
The Benefits of a Fully Functioning Integrated Master Plan

Remember meeting several prosperous yet dissatisfied individuals or couples in our Introduction?

There were:

- **The Sullivans**, who felt their lives lacked purpose and that they spent too much time meeting with their advisers
- **Max Hatfield**, whose father's lack of planning left him feeling lost, in addition to subjecting the estate to onerous taxes
- **Marjorie Lambert**, who struggled to understand her family's complex finances with little help from advisers who would not collaborate

We have seen the *Integrated Planning Process*™ energize families like the Sullivans who discover a new purpose in the *Goals Development Stage*.

The *Integrated Planning Process* can relieve the burden of some of the tax-related missteps made by Max Hatfield's father. Even more important to Max—it can ensure that he articulates his legacy for his family and equips them to handle the privileges and responsibilities of wealth.

Marjorie Lambert would save time and energy working with an integrated team of financial and legal advisers. She could delegate many of the routine procedures.

Each of these individuals would experience the Magic of a fully integrated financial, legal plan and life. It is never too late to benefit from the integrated planning power of your Master Plan.

The process described in this book—what we call a Family Legacy Journey—is not only about investments and legal documents. These are merely tools to use along the way. With careful planning and the help of your team you can guard against **dangers**, take advantage of **opportunities**, and reinforce the **strengths** of the people important to you and your family. Moreover, you can motivate and educate your junior family members so that they use the family wealth to enhance their ability to take their place in your family's future and promote harmony and good will as they benefit society with their many talents.

So what next? What if you would like to apply integrated financial and legal planning to your life? We suggest that you start by sharing this book with your primary advisers. They may welcome the opportunity to work more collaboratively with you and your other advisers.

We hope that in this book you have seen some aspect of your Family Legacy Journey. A quote widely attributed to Winston Churchill reminds us:

> "Every day you may make progress. Every step may be fruitful. Yet there will stretch out before you an ever-lengthening, ever-ascending, ever-improving path. You know you will never get to the end of the journey. But this, so far from discouraging, only adds to the joy and glory of the climb."

CHAPTER TEN

As you go forward, be bold as you call upon your resources.
You may find they will exceed your expectations
as they rise to your challenges.

Experience the benefits of an integrated plan;
one that is organized around your goals.

This process will result in a more enjoyable
and rewarding life for you and your family.

Afterward

We would enjoy hearing from you. Contact us with your feedback and suggestions about this book at:

- feedback@cpcll.com
- bwoodman@woodmaneaton.com
- mike@dkeinc.com

A Comment about Fees

To avoid misunderstandings, you and your advisers should be clear about how you will pay for their advice. Your arrangement should be spelled out in written contracts for services.

There are four main approaches, each of which can be appropriate under the right circumstances.

- **Commission-based.** Your adviser provides a significant amount of information, analysis, and education for no fee in the hope of making a commission on the sale of a product or products.
- **Hourly fees.** Fees are charged for the hours devoted to the planning.
- **Project fee.** A flat project fee is charged based on the professional's assessment of the complexity and scope of the engagement and the skill, judgment and expertise required.
- **Percentage of assets.** Fees are based on the value of assets managed or the value of the assets that are the subject of the planning.

Information about the Authors

History of the Authors' Collaboration

Byron Woodman and Michael Hartley began working together in 1997, providing integrated financial, legal and life plan evaluation, design and implementation for client families. They also participate in the ongoing maintenance, monitoring and governance for plans as members of teams providing The Family Board of Advisors services.

Byron has been interested in integrating financial, legal and life planning since he began his practice as an estate planning tax lawyer more than 30 years ago. In 1982, he formally developed an interdisciplinary team to provide such services.

When Byron met Mike nine years ago, he discovered Mike's ability to design and implement collaborative systems that serve the strategic needs of high net worth families.

Byron and Mike look forward to many more years of collaborating to help their clients fulfill their lifetime goals.

Byron E. Woodman, Jr., JD, LLM, AEP

Byron has practiced in the areas of estate planning and tax law since 1970. He founded Woodman & Eaton, P.C., an estate planning law firm, in Concord, Massachusetts in 1980. Prior to Woodman & Eaton, Byron was a partner in the Boston law firm of Sherburne, Powers & Needham.

Byron is a founder and Director of Monument Financial Advisors, LLC, a Registered Investment Advisor. He is also a founder and President of The Monument Group Fiduciaries, LLC, which provides supporting services to trustees and beneficiaries of trusts. From 1983 to 2004, he served as President and Director of Concord Equity Corporation, a Registered Investment Advisor. He serves as a director on private and public boards.

Michael T. Hartley, CFP, AAMS

Mike served as the President of Dale K. Ehrhart, Inc. (1992 to 2001), a Registered Investment Advisor, and currently serves as their Chairman and Chief Executive. He frequently works as a member of collegial teams that provide sophisticated estate, tax, and investment planning to individuals and families, as well as family office services.

In addition to his executive duties, Mike is involved on a day-to-day basis with the use of Modern Portfolio Theory concepts in portfolio design, derivative strategies to facilitate diversification of concentrated equity position and other forms of sophisticated investment planning. Prior to joining Dale K. Ehrhart, Inc. in 1985, Mike worked as a corporate comptroller and director of finance. He serves on and advises numerous private and public foundation and endowment boards.

Selected Readings

Annino, Patricia. *Women & Money: A Practical Guide to Estate Planning.* BookSurge Publishing, 2004.

Bradley, Susan with Mary Martin. *Sudden Money™: Managing a Financial Windfall.* New York: John Wiley & Sons, Inc., 2000.

Fithian, Scott. *Values-Based Estate Planning: A Step-by-Step Approach to Wealth Transfer for Professional Advisors.* John Wiley & Sons, 2000.

Gibson, John W. and Hartley, Bonnie Brown *The Dynamics of Aging Families.* Venice, FL.: Cambio Press, 2006.

Hartley, Bonnie Brown *Unexpected Wealth: A Fire Drill for Building Strength and Flexibility in Families.* Venice, FL.: Cambio Press, 2005.

Hartley, Bonnie Brown *Sudden Death: A Fire Drill for Building Strength and Flexibility in Families.* Venice, FL.: Cambio Press, 2005.

Hughes, James E. Jr. *Family Wealth—Keeping it in the Family: How Family Members and Their Advisers Preserve Human, Intellectual, and Financial Assets for Generations.* Bloomberg Press, 2004.

Katzenbach, Jon R. and Douglas K. Smith, *The Wisdom of Teams.* McKinsey & Company, Inc., 1993.

Sullivan, Dan and Catherine Nomura. *The Laws of Lifetime Growth: Always Make Your Future Bigger Than Your Past.* Berrett-Koehler Publications, 2006.

Williams, Roy and Vic Preisser. *Preparing Heirs: Five Steps to a Successful Transition of Family Wealth and Values.* Robert D. Reed, 2003.

Woodman, Byron E., III. QuestionsForLiving®. www.questionsforliving.com